THINKING ABOUT MEMOIR

Thinking
About Memoir

Abigail Thomas

New York / London
www.sterlingpublishing.com

For CTV

Passages from this book appeared first, in slightly
different form, in the *Washington Post Magazine*
and *The Iowa Review*.

Library of Congress Cataloging-in-Publication Data Available

10 9 8 7 6 5 4 3 2

Published by Sterling Publishing Co., Inc.
387 Park Avenue South, New York, N.Y. 10016
The AARP name and logo are registered trademarks of AARP,
used under license to Sterling Publishing Co., Inc.
Copyright © 2008 Abigail Thomas
Distributed in Canada by Sterling Publishing
c/o Canadian Manda Group, 165 Dufferin Street
Toronto, Ontario, Canada M6K 3H6
Distributed in the United Kingdom by GMC Distribution Services
Castle Place, 166 High Street, Lewes, East Sussex, England BN7 1XU
Distributed in Australia by Capricorn Link (Australia) Pty. Ltd.
P.O. Box 704, Windsor, NSW 2756, Australia

Sterling ISBN 978-1-4027-5235-3

For information about custom editions, special sales, premium and
corporate purchases, please contact Sterling Special Sales
Department at 800-805-5489 or
specialsales@sterlingpublishing.com.

CONTENTS

Preface

This is a book about writing memoir. It doesn't come with blueprints or a set of instructions—there aren't any. Memoir can consist of looking back at a single summer, or the span of a whole lifetime. The book is divided into sections that give it a professional look, but don't be fooled—the sections are leaky, and spill from one to another. This book is also about being in the here-and-now, because memories survive on a wisp of fragrance, or a particular shade of blue, or a song that reminds you of a song, and you don't want to miss anything. Keep your eyes and ears open, also your heart. This is about letting the mind open up and wander, and about letting one thing lead to another. Follow the details. Detail is the antidote to boredom, and it tends to keep depression at bay.

This book is also about the habit of writing as a way to keep track of what's going on in the front and the back of your mind. You can write about nothing in particular; just write. An embarrassingly trivial note in my diary this morning about the local coffee tossed me back to Blynn's on 14th Street in 1958. My friends and I went there every day after school to have serious conversations about I don't remember what, but we were fueled by cup after cup of black coffee. I remember the waitress calling out, "Adam and Eve on a raft, hold the raft." I remember the booths were cracked red vinyl, none of us ate much of anything, and I think we all smoked Kents, but I don't remember what the raft was. Now I remember a small perfect shell I wore on a silver chain in those days. For the first time in ages I remember I buried that shell with a baby. One thing leads to another, like it or not.

Memoir is the story of how we got here from there. I hope this book will inspire different ways to look at the moment you're in right now, and see how far back it can take you. I hope it will make you admire how surprising life is, and I hope you will write.

Because who knows where that raft is going. Somebody's got to jump aboard.

THINKING ABOUT MEMOIR

one

Writing Memoir

How to get started, how to keep going. What is memoir? How do you write one? What if you can't remember anything, or worse, what if you remember it all? What do you put in? Who do you want your readers to be? I can't write personal stuff, you say, my family will be upset. You have to put those worries aside. You need to feel free to write about the uncomfortable truths, and unless your motive for writing is revenge, you may find that these moments of discomfort are mostly your own. But, you say, I know so much about life now. I want to share my thoughts with all English-speaking peoples, and if lucky, foreign rights will also be sold. A word of caution: If you want to impart wisdom, you might wind up with a 300-page greeting card.

Writing memoir is a way to figure out who you used to be and how you got to be who you are. Still, as Raymond Carver once said, "What good is insight? It only makes things worse." Why dredge up a lot of dusty memories? Why remind yourself that the old days will never come back? Why remind yourself of your own mortality? (The word *memory* comes from the same root as the word *mourn*, and that should tell you something.) You will find there are many reasons to go look in the icebox, or turn on the television, or reread *Middlemarch*. But pay attention to the little voice that whispers, "This part was interesting." Pay attention to everything.

Recently I bought a garden statue of the Virgin Mary. I am not a religious person, but her face is beautiful, her blue robe faded, her manner full of grace. I put it in the living room, not wanting her rained on. A friend, Helen Klein Ross, looked at her and smiled. "I used to stare at her when I was little," she said, "hoping to see movement." She paused, brightened. "Because then I would be a saint!" If Helen hadn't already written brilliantly about her upbringing in a large Catholic family in the

Midwest, I'd have said, "Helen! Start right there! Write!"

But the jumping-off place isn't always so obvious. You can't always find the way in. Sometimes you need a side door. That's where the exercises come in. Here's the one I give all my writing students the first week of the class.

Take any ten years of your life, reduce them to two pages, and every sentence has to be three words long—not two, not four, but three words long. You discover there's nowhere to hide in three-word sentences. You discover that you can't include everything, but half of writing is deciding what to leave out. Learning what to leave out is not the same thing as putting in only what's important. Sometimes it's what you're not saying that gives a piece its shape. And it's surprising what people include. Marriage, divorce, love, sex—yes, there's all of that, but often what takes up precious space is sleeping on grass, or an ancient memory of blue Popsicle juice running down your sticky chin. When you're done, run your mind over everything the way a safecracker sandpapers his fingers to feel the clicks. If there is one sentence that hums, or gives off sparks, you've hit the jackpot. Then write another two pages starting right there.

Another exercise: Write two pages about a time when you were dressed inappropriately for the occasion. What occasion? Who thought you were inappropriate? That's up to you.

A woman wrote about her first husband's death, which had happened maybe twenty years ago. He was helping somebody load a truck, a favor for somebody he barely knew—that's the kind of generous man he was. The truck moved unexpectedly and he was thrown to the ground, and sustained a head injury so severe that when they got him to the emergency room he was declared brain-dead. Hours later she was standing on the roof of the hospital with her husband's brother, deciding whether or not to take him off life support. She was wearing flip-flops, shorts, and a T-shirt and she remembers thinking how these were the wrong clothes to be wearing at such a moment. She had never written about his death before. Focusing on what she was wearing gave her the distance.

A side door.

I give assignments in my writing classes because it's hard to make something up out of a clear blue sky. Two pages is all I ask, and it doesn't have to be a story.

It doesn't have to be an anything. It can contain a character who shows up out of breath. It can contain a lake and a bunch of swans. There can be conversation or silence. It can take place entirely in the dark. I have learned we do better when we're not trying too hard—there is nothing more deadening to creativity than the grim determination to write. At the very least, assignments can provide a writer with a nicely stocked larder, and some notion of where the mind goes when it's off its leash. And once in a while, if we're lucky, an assignment helps you find that side door into a story you've been staring too directly in the eye.

Ideas for assignments come from everywhere. I sit down on the train and all around me people are whipping out their cell phones.

"Bob? Bob? Bob? Bob?"

"Alan? Alan? Alan? Alan?"

"Joyce?"

And then once we clear the tunnel I hear everybody saying, "I'm on the train." Well, I'm on the train too, but so what?

Write two pages in which someone keeps her temper in check.

I do a lot of involuntary eavesdropping on the train. Last week I overheard a young woman who talked all the way from Poughkeepsie to Penn Station on her cell phone. She had an emergency, she said. She needed three platters delivered in the next two hours to a party her boss was throwing. Somebody had forgotten to order food.

"I'll pay any amount of money," she said. "Yes, such a rush, I understand. . . . It's like ten people . . . I need three platters. . . . Do you have tapas? No? Chorizo? . . . you know, those Mexican sausages? Oh . . . how about Greek with stuffed . . . oh . . . I understand. . . ." The negotiations went badly with one deli after another and she kept getting cut off, and then she finally found someone who would do it. "Oh, thank you so . . . okay, thank you very—" Then silence. Then she must have called her office: "I'm just jumping in the shower, I'm still downtown. . . . yes, better today . . ."

But that wasn't the end. She called the deli back with one last request: Don't send it until she called. She needed to be the person to open the door and receive the food because her boss had wanted it delivered from Food Emporium and she wanted to get it out of the boxes before her boss arrived. So after an hour and ten minutes of negotiations she was going to get off at Penn Station, call the deli, and race to East 68th Street to receive three platters of cheese.

*Write two pages in which someone obsesses
over something meaningless.*

The pact we make My husband, Rich, lost his memory after he was hit by a car and suffered traumatic brain injury. In a moment of perfect clarity he once described his loss like this: "Pretend you are walking up the street with your friend. You are looking in windows. But right behind you is a man with a huge paint roller filled with white paint and he is painting over everywhere you've been, erasing everything. He erases your friend. You don't even remember his name." It's terrifying. Because who are we without five minutes ago? Who are we without our stories? Where is the continuum of consciousness? Is it all one big lily pad of a moment? I can't remember five minutes ago either, most likely, but I still (usually) have a sense of time passing, and if I look out the window I pretty much know what time of day it is, what season. I can locate myself in time and place. Even if I can't find my glasses or remember what I read this morning or can't for the life of me figure out what I'm doing in the kitchen, I am still a consciousness aware of her surroundings.

What did Rich know? He stared for a long time at a photograph of himself, and his brother, and an old friend, taken maybe sixty-five years ago. I don't know what went through his mind. Perhaps he wasn't thinking, perhaps he was absorbing. There are notebooks he wrote a few things in when he first got hurt, trying to figure things out, things that made no sense to him. It's what I do too.

Writing is the way I ground myself, and it's what keeps me sane. Writing is the way I try and make sense of my life, try to find meaning in accident, reasons why what happens happens—even though I know that why is a distraction, and meaning you have to cobble together yourself. Sometimes just holding a pen in my hand and writing *milk butter eggs sugar* calms me. Truth is what I'm ultimately after, truth or clarity. I think that's what we're all after, truth, although I'd never have said such a thing when I was young. And I write nonfiction because you can't get away with anything when it's just you and the page. No half-truths, no cosmetics. What would be the point?

Why bother writing at all? Once in a while you come too close to a nerve, and your writing goes flat, and your first thought might be to change the subject. But this is the most interesting of moments. There is so much to be found out.

Hiding behind that paragraph is probably something worth knowing. You can stare at the page and realize, "Hot dog—this is a safe to be cracked!", or you can crawl under the covers and take a nice nap.

So remember: The writer of memoir makes a pact with her reader that what she writes is the truth as best she can tell it. But the original pact, the real deal, is with herself. Be honest, dig deep, or don't bother.

two

The Habit of Writing

Good writing habits A lot of writing consists of waiting around for the aquarium to settle so you can see the fish. Walking around muttering seems to hasten the process. Taking public transportation nowhere helps. Looking out the bus window lets the back of your mind move forward. Don't listen to anything but natural sound. Don't look at anything you have to turn on. This is about the pleasure of silence. This is not meditating; this is reacquainting yourself with yourself. Something interesting might enter your head if you let it alone. We are bombarded by media. We are overstimulated these days. We talk too much.

So there are the hours of mulling, stewing, allowing the mind to let down its guard, but the rest of it is the writing part. It helps to be in the daily habit of scribbling stuff down. I suggest you go to the stationery store and pick out a notebook you actually like. Take your time. This is going to be your companion for a while. I love blank moleskin. I believe the writer Bruce Chatwin bought them 200 at a time before taking off on a journey. Then choose a pen that you find pleasant to write with. Buy two of them. (If you buy ten, they will all be lost within an hour.) I like the kind with a point like a needle, and for me the dragging of a sharp pen across a page is a sensual experience. And, more important, I feel as if I'm actually doing something. You can't whip out your laptop on the crowded number one train at rush hour, but you can probably get to your notebook when you hear something you want to remember, or glimpse a memory of the kind that vanish so quickly. I once observed a father holding his son on his lap and the little boy sat straight up, like a vase of flowers. I wrote it down, although it went nowhere (until now).

Call it a diary—it is less imposing than a journal, which sounds like an end in itself. I steer clear of the word *journal*—and its spawn, the verb *to journal,* as in, "I have been journaling all my life." If I were to call my notebook a journal I would probably write with the notion that it be published someday, preferably posthumously, and people would marvel. This would make me self-conscious. I would be trying to perfect each sentence before its time. I prefer notes; if I clean it up too fast I lose the spark. Everything goes in: grocery lists, things to do (so I can scratch them off) random observations, knitting patterns, recipes, overheard dialogue, everything. A diary isn't sacred. Think of it as the written equivalent of singing in the shower. I don't care what I'm writing and I don't pay any attention to language. Most of what's in there is boring, but it keeps me in the habit. Writing doesn't have to be good, not at first.

By now I am addicted: I need to feel my hand scribbling across a page. A friend wanted to know what I was working on; she was reading the paper and I was writing in my diary. We were having coffee at Bread Alone.

"Nothing," I said.

"It can't be nothing," she said, assuming perhaps that writers were always doing something interesting. She leaned over and read, "It is taking a long time to get my sandwich."

Case closed.

Write two pages of uninspiring diary entries (to break the ice).

Write two pages, the second sentence of which is "It's not funny."

👆

Rules of diary keeping Don't read anyone else's.

Don't leave yours lying around. There should be stuff in your diary that is nobody's business but your own.

👆

Notes from a diary Speaking of aquariums, a young friend of mine got married, and her husband came with a big fish tank. I guess there were a bunch of fish to start, but at the time of the story there were only two left, Big Boy and Little Girl. The aquarium was dirty, because these fish like murk, they are cave dwellers, they like to hide. They are bright red-gold, and I can just see the glint of their bodies appearing and disappearing into the murk, like those thoughts you can never carry all the way to consciousness. My friend wasn't crazy about the fish, but her husband had had them a long time. My friend wanted to put a piano where the giant fish tank stood. From time to time her husband brought home small fish and dumped them into the water. A day or two would go by and he'd look at the aquarium and remark, "Not so many anymore." Little Girl had had thousands of babies over her lifetime. She spent all her time now in the cave my friend's husband built for her in a corner of the aquarium. Then one day my friend noticed a commotion in the tank. Big Boy had somehow lured Little Girl out of her cave and now he was pounding the life out of her in a corner of the tank. The male has a hump on his head, the better to fight with. Little Girl was dying, my friend saw, and she called for her husband who came and got the old fish out of the water and into a pail of water and put her in the laundry room. Then he went back about his chores, mowing the lawn, I think. "But you can't leave her in there to die alone," my friend said, but perhaps he was already out the door. So my friend sat in the laundry room and kept Little Girl company, noticing that as she died the fish got grayer and grayer until finally she floated on top of the water. I don't know what to do with this story, or why it affects me as it does. Later I looked up these fish, and after the descriptions of habitat and feeding and reproducing and so forth came the heading "Nature" and the word beneath was "beware." I tell this story because I had my notebook handy at the time, and got it all down. I tell this story here because

I have nowhere else to tell it. I tell this story because it made me love my friend even more. Sometimes writing is a way to offer a reader someone to love.

Write two pages about a time when you felt compassion unexpectedly.

Also on the subject of fish: My mother tells me that the first thing my father checked for when I was born was a gill. This is because he had a gill, a tiny hole at the top of one ear, vestigial, but he was proud to find I had one too.

Write two pages about a physical characteristic you are proud to have inherited or passed on.

A friend remembers an old girlfriend who spent a large part of every day in the bathtub holding her breath underwater. Why? I asked. He didn't know. Maybe she was reproducing the moment when we lost our gills and breathed air for the first time, bursting from the surface of the water joyfully, explosively, and taking a big gulp: Eons of rehearsing for that one moment of spontaneity. That's what taking notes and then the act of writing is like, come to think of it.

Write two pages of whatever you remember about something being born.

Now I remind you that this all came from having had a diary handy, and that it went into the diary in rough notes, which were fun to make nice afterward, when I'd had a chance to think. Or let the aquarium settle. One of these days I'll figure out what to do with it.

Write two pages that take place in water.

Diary as fact checker From time to time my daughter Jen looks at her old diaries. She kept a pretty accurate record of growing up in the seventies, most of which I don't want to hear. "Don't tell me! Don't tell me!" I want to shout when she reads me passages over the phone. But there are hilarious bits, too. "I decided I don't want to see Bobby in the daytime anymore. I noticed a lot of icky things. His teeth are gross, he's got acne . . . he's got a wart and a tiny little beard and all these things just get me so depressed." Another day: "I dreamed me and Bobby were in the bedroom and mommy came in looking really mean and she shot me and cut off my head and sent it to Bobby in a hatbox." This is not all that funny, it is horrifying—perhaps it's the use of the word "mommy" that makes me laugh, albeit nervously, and I wonder why I feel guilty for something I did in someone else's dream.

Write two pages of apologizing for something you didn't do.

"I'm not driving you to school just because it's your birthday," she has a record of my saying once.

"Oh, surely not," I protest, rifling through my scrappy memory for extenuating circumstances. A broken toe? Sick baby? No gas?

"And it was raining," Jen continues, delivering the coup de grâce.

I can't argue. She had no reason to make anything up. It was a diary after all, not a story.

Write two pages of something you can't deny.

Mysterious old diary entry I have just come across these instructions printed neatly in an old diary: Hang up-press function/edit up or down then scroll to ringer setting then press arrow to right select desired volume using up or down arrow. Base unit press.

At the bottom of this page I describe emptying a sugar bowl on somebody's head. I don't know whether these were notes for a story, or if I really did it, saying, "Sweets to the sweet," as my diary records.

Write two pages of something you wrote or did that you no longer understand.

Write two pages of "sweets to the sweet."

Diary as a means of keeping myself honest I am keeping track of what I am not buying and writing it in my diary:

> *No butterfly bushes.*
>
> *No hollyhocks.*
>
> *No pigs' ears.*
>
> *No cotton pajamas.*
>
> *No hair lightener.*
>
> *No curtains.*
>
> *No out-of-season organic blueberries.*
>
> *No Syro-Hittite bird goddess from 1200 bc.*
>
> *No hand-painted wooden pigs.*

No Victorian photos of house and occupants in Indiana, reminiscent of the house in In Cold Blood.

No organic futon mattress with pine frame.

No trilobites.

No illuminated manuscript from 1791.

Last Saturday however, before I turned over my new leaf, I went to The Golden Notebook and bought Stanley Kunitz's *Collected Poems* even though I'm pretty sure I already have a copy some-where. (*What makes the engine run / desire desire desire*). I bought *Water for Elephants* by Sara Gruen and two more copies of *Mystery and Manners* by Flannery O'Connor, one for a friend. Later I bought two newspapers, a pound of hamburger, hamburger rolls, and diet dog food. I bought two pots of pink hollyhocks. I bought creeping thyme ground cover (quite a lot of it) and three pots of daylilies. I bought pink pansies. I bought the new moleskin notebook in which I am recording this. I bought two new pens. I bought a desk organizer. I brought all the stuff home with me in my car.

The only items still to come through the post office are one nun box made by the same artist as made my shark box, one large painting of flowers and a dinosaur by Mose Tolliver, one two-drawer box made out of an old packing crate, one movie from Amazon.com but I can't remember which one, one sculpture of a woodpecker on a branch twenty-eight inches long by outsider artist Ralph Griffin, and one copy of *Lost:* Season Two bought on the black market, which is coming from England. I already received the plug-in waterfall scene that lights and ripples. I didn't bid on the Royal Doulton Bunnykins mug. I am not bidding on the huge tramp-art log-cabin jewelry box.

Shark box? It is a diorama fourteen by eight by three inches in which numerous small plastic grooms have been eaten or are being eaten by sharks. Several bloody grooms lie on the ground. One faces the wall. Big sharks are painted on the backdrop. One groom's head is completely inside the jaws of a real plastic shark. "The grooms are vintage," said the maker. I bought it for thirty-five dollars but would have spent more. "It's great, Mom," said one daughter, "but I don't understand why you bought it." Ah, how to answer? "I had to have it," is all I can say. The nun box has no sharks.

Write two pages of what you had to have.

Yesterday I went to the post office at five o'clock to pick up a package. I stood behind the red line until it was my turn to approach the desk, holding my postal package claim slip in front of me like a convict with her serial number. The clerk who is usually so jovial took it and frowned. I heard him say, "Blah blah blah you should be fired from the Woodstock Post Office." I didn't pay much attention. I was wondering what I'd bought because I'd gotten to the point of being surprised whenever I opened a package. "There's a lot of stuff going to your house all the time." He was glaring at me. "All the time. A *lot* of stuff."

"You're not kidding," I heard myself say as if I were the passive recipient, as shocked and put out as he. I signed the receipt and gathered up my huge misshapen package (which turned out to contain the *Large Wildcat* by Mose Tolliver) and retreated to my car, unmasked—the bright red compulsive shopper. Once last year the UPS guy asked if I was opening a store, but he was in a good mood. I went home and counted up the things to come from eBay and paid UPS rate to save further embarrassment at the post office. And I stopped shopping, just like that.

Write two pages of humiliating exposure.

My friend Denise tells me somebody told her, "Shopping is despair," but my daughter Jennifer says,

"Shopping is hope." Hope gets out of hand. One turquoise ring from eBay is not enough. I must have five. A single secondhand Coach bag is not satisfying—I bid on seven. As I have implied, one is not a concept I understand. When I smoked I smoked three packs a day, when I drank, well, let's not get into that. If your psyche is a balloon animal and you squeeze to eliminate the cigarettes and whiskey, the crazy has to go somewhere. A friend's mother ate nothing but clams for six months. Morning, noon, and night, nothing but clams. "I don't know what it is—I can't seem to get enough of them," she told her son. He shakes his head, but I understand. I eat nothing but broccoli for a month, then yogurt for six days, then (for one glorious week) lamb chops. One day I roasted a chicken and had seven chicken sandwiches before nightfall. If I like something, I like it a lot. Just one doesn't cut it. I don't know what it is I can't get enough of.

At least I don't have shopping bags full of duck sauce.

Write two pages of what you have too much of.

Today I resist buying June and Johnny singing together. I resist hopping in the car to find a carpet store and pick out carpeting for my naked stairs even though I am experiencing a surge of positive energy to go do that right now. How comforting the look and feel of carpeted stairs. I would choose dark rich colors in a flowered pattern. It would be like the carpet in Grandma Thomas's house, and I would recall how the gas fire in her fireplace danced blue and yellow and smelled like heat. She fried lamb chops. She boiled her coffee with an eggshell to trap the bitter oils. Her Christmas tree lights were little flames. When she died we lived in New Orleans. My mother whispered, "Go tell your father you're sorry." My father flew to Flushing for the funeral. He never said a word. Grandpa Thomas went downhill from there.

In New Orleans I spent all my allowance on blue Popsicles, which I ate one after another, my forearm sticky with juice. Our family lived at 51A Macalaster Place on the campus of Tulane University. The road was paved with white shells, and when it rained water overflowed the curbs, rushed into the grass for a little while, and sank away again. I remember my little sister Judy and I caught hundreds of doodlebugs and dragged them around in a wagon. Then we bashed them with a rock. Movies were a nickel on Saturdays but we didn't have to pay, and most of the movies starred June Allyson. When we moved to Minnesota I bought 25 red lollipops with my allowance.

Sometimes I bought a bar of white Turkish taffy and fifteen red lollipops. Once in a while a nickel's worth of licorice. Those were simple times. When you got money, you spent it on sugar and when you got old, you died.

Write two pages of how you spent your allowance.

In Minnesota at the university they had a cow with a hole in its stomach. I don't think we had to pay to see it, but memory puts 50 cents in my hand and then we were ushered into the dark barn. They took a blanket off the cow's back and there was this big hole, and you could see the hay turning over and over inside, kind of like a dryer. The cow just stood there swishing her tail. It was sad and fascinating. We lived at 1488 Branston Street and our telephone number was MIdway 8-8237. I had a fossil collection and some petrified wood. I had a misshapen root that resembled a squirrel frozen in a death rictus and I brandished this about when friends came over. I had a big pink rabbit onto whose back I tied all my other stuffed animals and then hopped the pink rabbit to safety. We moved in 1956 and my father, who was packing the house, left everything behind.

Write two pages of what got left behind.

I do not collect cows because they scare the shit out of me. I have a large collection of wooden horses.

Write two pages of what you do not collect.

Recently my friend had a birthday and I bought him a beach chair and a blue shirt.

Today—July 29, 2006—I am not buying:

> *An 1870 copper horse and sulky weathervane.*
>
> *A rare early sewer tile basset hound fourteen inches long.*
>
> *A large carved and painted wooden tooth trade sign for a dentist measuring seventeen by ten inches.*

In other words, I have stopped shopping. Maybe I will send the post office guy a note.

The tooth is big enough to use as an ottoman.

Looking back, I knew I was in trouble when I stopped opening the boxes. I still have not unwrapped one painting (unknown); one queen-size EuroBed bought for forty-eight dollars; two sets of pale blue queen-size sheets, 440 thread count, bought for twenty-two dollars; something in a big box I don't know what it is; something else in a medium box I don't know what it is. In the laundry room is another thin box I hid on a shelf next to the detergent like an alcoholic with her whiskey, I don't know what's in that either.

Write two pages of when you knew you were in trouble.

The tooth is carved from a single block of wood and is very heavy. It is in good untouched condition with minor age cracks, some staining, and a chip on the bottom of one root. They are asking five hundred dollars and the auction will be over in six hours and forty-one minutes. To show how big, there is a Coke can in front. The tooth has provenance. I could hang it in my window. My teeth are stained and cracked and one in the back is tipping over like an old ferry piling. It lost its mate years ago and there is nothing to go up against. Also, it broke in half when I was eating spaghetti. The dentist wanted to fix it but I protested. "No patient of mine is going to walk around with a tooth like that," he said merrily, and made me an appointment that I didn't keep. That was six years ago when I lived in the city.

Thought: In New York City nobody cares how many packages you get.

The seller of the tooth has sold 1,114 objects and his approval rating is 99.6 positive. I have bought 141 objects and have a 98.6 positive rating. This is because I complained about a Coach bag that dyed my hands black. And once, inexplicably, I didn't pay for six miniature bowling pins I'd won for three dollars. They were two inches tall.

There are now five hours and three minutes left to bid on the tooth. I have viewed it from four angles. Upside down it looks like an unfriendly flower. There is a similar tooth in the collection at the Shelburne Museum, which is included in the National Gallery of Art's folk art catalog from 1987. This is its provenance. None of this means squat to me because these are not reasons for bidding on a big wooden tooth. The reason is that you fall in love and absolutely have to have it this minute. One week, I bid on and won twenty-two Persian rugs, but that was years ago.

My sisters sometimes spy on me by looking at my recent purchases.

The tooth goes for $713.37 at the last minute. The person who bought the tooth also recently bought a folksy painted birdhouse, three balls of wound-up rags, and a street sign. This person also bought a "funky hand-carved foot, reddish color," eight inches long, for $110. Now he has a foot and a tooth. Checking further, this person bought a painted wooden penguin whose image is, alas, no longer available. I get quickly off the Web site, lest I lose my resolve and bid on the 1674 map of the United States with California as an island, although I am in much more danger from the rare midcentury sewer tile figural lion doorstop. What I love is the worn smile on its face. It's a how-did-I-get-here? sort of smile, a how-lucky-to-be-a-lion-instead-of-just-a-plain-sewer-tile philosophical sort of smile.

There are no bids on this object so far, and I have six days to think it over.

Write two pages of restraint.

Write two pages of how did I get here? and the accompanying facial expression(s).

three

Memory

Imperfect memory My sister remembers many things I have forgotten: the sundial, the pear tree, and the pear picker (which she says I lost). The pear picker comes back to me now—a long pole with pincers at one end to cut the pears and a net to catch them. What she remembers goes into her pile, so the pear picker belongs to my sister now. Her pile is bigger than mine; my memory is full of holes. But I can still see the tree; it hung out over a bend in the road, dropping pears all fall until the road was slippery and sweet. Yellow jackets hung around, cranky and unpredictable, and we walked on the other side.

I don't bring up the precious stuff unless I'm certain I'm right, because getting something wrong is even worse than forgetting it entirely. I remember a waterfall in the woods and the deep cold pool it fell into. I think a grape arbor stood above it, held up by fluted columns. But I could be mistaken. "No, there was no arbor over the pool," I imagine my sister saying, and I am banished from the garden, covered only by my small scrap of memory. Still, I can't go back and knock down the columns and yank out the vines. Even if I tried, it would put itself back together again, the way I've always remembered it.

I don't know why some things stick in my mind and not others. I recall, for instance, one long family trip when my sister and I amused ourselves by tearing limb from limb two plastic dolls we disliked. I remember how satisfying it was to throw the arms and legs out the car windows, and then the two heads, and finally the torsos. I don't know if she remembers any of this, and I don't know why I do except perhaps for what we'd named the dolls: Toenail and Fingernail.

But there was another car trip. This time we were driving to Maine, and the road was lonely and the sky the blackest I'd ever seen and my sister and I were in the backseat. She was just a little girl, two or three, which makes me four or five, and she must have leaned against a door that hadn't closed

properly because she fell out of the car. I remember
tapping my parents on the shoulders and saying,
"Judy isn't in the car anymore," and it taking some
time before they paid attention. I don't remember
the frantic drive back to find her, but I seem to
recall a darkened house and my father, my sister in
his arms, banging on the door to wake the inhabi-
tants. I vividly remember, whether I saw it or not, a
small white sink filling up with my little sister's
blood. Her head had cracked open. She still gets
bad headaches from that accident, although it happened more than sixty years ago.

Recently she told me that I pushed her out of the
car. There was no rancor in her tone, it was just a
statement. We were in her apartment, it was an ordinary afternoon. We had been chatting idly. I was
shocked.

"I did not push you," I said, but she didn't reply.
I don't know if she was teasing, and I am afraid to
press her. What if she insisted? What if she really
believed it? "You're wrong," I would want to say. "I
would remember such a terrible thing."

I would remember, wouldn't I?

Wouldn't I?

Conflicting memories I struck up my courage and showed the memory piece to my sister.

1) The pear picker did not have pincers, although it did have a net. "You did not lose it," she said. "You left it in the street and it got run over."

2) There was no grape arbor over the pool ("Think about the grapes dropping in," she said). The arbor was down by the river. Maybe I clumped everything together for efficiency's sake? Perhaps I wanted my treasures in one box.

3) We were not driving to Maine, but somewhere in Baltimore. She was not two or three, she was four. It was not nighttime, it was day. Nighttime, lonely country road in Maine, darkened farmhouse—was my memory making its own story?

4) The last question I couldn't bring myself to ask her, but my youngest sister did. "Did Abby really push you out of the car?" she asked. "I was joking," was the answer. Phew.

Write two pages of a fading memory—
something you have to squint to see.

Memory in the making The first day of January my husband died and toward the end of the month I went to Belize with my best friend Chuck to visit a pal, Ann, who had a free house on the beach. Blue everything, blue blue blue. And green. The tree next to the porch had leaves as big and round as lily pads and at night the moon shone silver all over them, like spilled mercury. Everything was beautiful and we were far away. We had no telephone. I saw frigate birds, my husband's favorite, or a bird I assigned as his favorite, and it seemed that whenever I thought of Rich, a frigate bird appeared in the sky overhead. I cried. But pelicans are my favorite birds and there were lots of them, smashing into the water for fish, and then later, hanging their heavy wings out to dry like gray laundry. I love that pelicans have no table manners, no grace. It's all about the food.

We ate fryjack for breakfast with honey and jam, we had butt bacon and eggs and fresh papaya and pineapple. We had lobster and shrimp and even though I don't drink anymore I had two delicious Belizean beers one night. We bounced around in a rusty truck on red dirt roads and when it failed to start, learned how to jump it with a screwdriver from two young men we met in the parking lot of the bank. People were friendly. One morning, due to an accident of light, I mistook a slope of the sand for the sea, and was startled when two big black dogs loped across what I took to be the horizon. My god, I thought, what kind of place is this?

We hired a fishing boat to take us to the big barrier reef, and landed on an island a little bigger than my living room. There were a couple of palms, a beat-up picnic table, and a grill. The water close to shore was the color of very expensive gin, because the sand was so white, and I spent a lot of time in that. Chuck and Ann went snorkeling out past where the big drop happens, but thank god I never mastered the art of breathing and the flippers were pretty much beyond me so I contented myself sticking close to shore. I saw some small fish and lots of what I think were sponges, some sea fans of a rosy magenta so beautiful I didn't believe my eyes—having no receptors for a color that fantastic. I wasn't sorry not to swim with schools of fish, or frolic with a bunch of dolphins, I didn't mind missing sharks or barracudas or any of the other awful possibilities open to us. When Chuck and Ann decided to swim far out to a big rock where waves were breaking and the snorkeling might be even better, I said nope, I'd drown and pull them down with me. And Cagey, the fisherman, who wanted to fish, took me farther out to sea. It was scary. I kept thinking, "Please don't fall out of the boat because I won't know how to get you back in," but he didn't.

On the way back to the mainland, my friend Chuck slipped and fell in the boat. He didn't complain, which worried me. Instead, he changed the subject of *How are you? Are you all right?* by wondering if it was water or sand that had wrecked his digital camera.

"What's in there?" I asked, because I knew it wasn't film.

"A memory card," he said. When I looked blank, he boiled it down for me—something he's good at. "It's just little bits of information."

One morning, in the lone tall palm at one end of the beach, there appeared a single buzzard. In the afternoon, I noticed the buzzard was standing on a little spit of sand at Rum Point. He was leaning toward the ocean, and he never moved. I wondered was he waiting for something delicious to wash up at his feet, but decided he was scanning the horizon, waiting for his mate to come back. "His own true love," were the words I used to myself.

"You've got to hand it to him," I said to Ann. "He hasn't budged in an hour. He hasn't even moved his head. That is one patient bird."

"I don't think that is a bird," she said. "It doesn't have a head."

So I set off down the beach. My buzzard turned out to be a long bleached stick around which a black garbage bag had gotten tangled. I don't know why I wasn't disappointed; maybe being blown together with random bits of trash made it even more buzzardlike. I asked Chuck to take its picture, but so far he hasn't sent it on.

Memory seems to be an independent creature inspired by event, not faithful to it. Maybe memory is what the mind does with its free time, decorating itself. Maybe it's like cave paintings. The thing is, I'm old enough now to know that the past is every bit as unpredictable as the future, and that memory, mine anyway, is not a faithful record of anything, and truth is not an absolute.

But I'm not talking about making things up out of whole cloth. We are all allowed a flourish or two—if it was day not night, and Baltimore not Maine, well, there's a reason why I remember it like that. But there's a difference between premeditated embellishment and the way memory works. There's a difference between lying and telling the truth. But do not despair.

We all know the difference.

I have a feeling that if I remember anything about Belize in twenty years, only the buzzard will make the cut. And I will remember him on his little spit of sand looking out to sea, waiting for his own true love to return.

Write two pages of mistaking something for something else.

⚓

Total recall Thank god I am not cursed with total recall. I can see myself stuck inside my steel trap of a memory, rattling the bars, hoping something would shake loose, some scrap I could look at all by itself, something to free me up. Life isn't a puzzle that needs to fit together perfectly, every piece locking into place with every other piece to form a perfect whole. Life is complicated. Stuff overlaps. Some stuff will never fit into one place. Where, for instance, do you stick embarrassment? How do you confine your sense of humor? Memoir is not about perfect accuracy of recording—it's more about finding perspective.

Is there one image or object that appears over and over in your memories? I don't know what baked Indian pudding is doing alongside certain terrible moments, but I know that stirring at the stove is a meditative activity for me. My mind can go elsewhere, while I stir the spoon round and round making circles, ellipses, parabolas, keeping the stuff smooth, keeping it moving so as not to burn the bottom. Adding more butter when nobody is looking. I could probably do a five-page riff on the meaning of dessert (I won't).

Is there something that crops up when you cast your mind back? A color? A taste? Write about it. What do you always see in your mind's eye? What is painted on the walls of your cave? A fireplace? A flat tire? A red hat? A black comb? Take whatever it is and write about it until you can't write anymore, then take a breath, walk around the block, and write some more.

Physical memories (textures) I was trying to recall the softest thing and remembered a white ermine muff. It might have been something that belonged to my grandmother, and how I loved to lay my cheek against it, but touching was not enough. Maybe this was my first experience of wanting to consume an object, to make it part of me. This may or may not have some psychological significance.

When my daughter Catherine was in her mid-twenties she saw a red patent-leather purse, a clutch purse with little tiny straps. I press her for details on this cold spring morning. When exactly did you see it? Where was it? Where were you? She can't remember exactly when or where. Only that she fell in love with it, so shiny and red. It was six inches tall, she thinks, and four inches wide. She thinks it might have been in Bendel's. It wasn't enough to possess the bag, although it was too expensive to consider buying.

"I wanted to *be* the bag," she said.

Write two pages about the thing you wanted to be.

Write two pages about the softest thing.

Sometimes all you have to do is open a jar. The smell of Noxzema takes me back to the summer of 1957, and the front seat of the old Hudson my boyfriend drove, and how we parked at the Amagansett beach at night and made out like crazy, and afterward I was afraid I was pregnant, even though we didn't do anything but kiss. The fear and the pleasure are as fresh to me every time I smell the stuff, and I keep a jar around so I can remember being young. So hunt down your mother's favorite perfume or your father's shaving cream. See where those scents take you.

When my daughter Catherine smells a cake of Cashmere Bouquet she is delivered back to her grandmother's apartment in New York City. She remembers Nonnie cooking her lamb chops for supper. She can recall the portrait that hung in the dark living room, a painting of her Nonnie as a beautiful young woman, and she can remember the fights over who should get it after Nonnie died— and how anger revealed the inner workings of a family. One specific detail always leads to another. When in doubt, don't go abstract. Stick to detail, and your story will begin to tell itself. You don't have to know where this is taking you. You don't have to know anything.

Where did you learn to smoke? How did you learn to dance? Did you go to dancing school? I did, driven there with whips and chains, and the only boy who volunteered to dance with me had been struck by lightning once, and had no eyelashes. Who was the first person you slow-danced with? I taught myself how to do the dirty bop in my bedroom listening to Carl Perkins sing "Blue Suede Shoes" while in the room below my parents tried to read. There was a very good-looking boy I used to see on summer vacation at the Amagansett beach, he did the bop and I wanted to dance with him the following summer. I had all winter to practice and I got good, but alas, the next July he told me I danced too dirty and he walked away.

Write two pages in which you got the wrong reaction from someone you hoped to impress.

Useless memories "A gentleman never wears brown." My English friend was fifteen. I was sixteen. He spoke with the considerable authority of an upper-class accent. I have always assumed he meant solid brown; I think tweed was okay. It is now fifty years later but whenever I see a man wearing a brown suit, I conclude instantly that this poor guy is no gentleman. It's the first and only thing I think of.

When I think of all I have forgotten, it seems absurd that this statement took up permanent residence inside my head. Of all the interesting or funny things my English friend has said, that is what stays with me. (My mother was fond of this remark of his: "Nasty chaps, the Tudors. Crafty, grasping . . . " But I remember that only because my mother did.)

Maybe it's because the sentence scans: a GENtleman NEver wears BROWN, and I know this is a poetic form I can't remember the name of. It goes along with a line from a bottle of wine that represents another rarely encountered poetic form I also forget the name of: "BOTtled in BRILliant conDItion but CARE must be USED in deCANting."

Write two pages of a useless sentence that stays in your head.

Write two pages of a snobbism you can't get rid of.

Memories of holidays Pick a holiday. Pick a month.

I have always hated Valentine's Day. Perhaps *hate* is too strong a word. *Felt uneasy* might be more like it. It started in school. We had colored paper, scissors, and an infinity of doilies that peeled off a single doily. We had snow falling in the dark outside the windows. We had a bucket of the good kind of paste, library paste, which I ate when no one was looking. The school radiators clanked and hissed. The room smelled of varnish and steam. Our scissors were blunt and the stakes were high—how many valentines would we get back? But we peeled and pasted and cut and wrote to our parents: "Be My Valentine." Store-bought valentines were what we gave one another—you got 100 in a cellophane bag for 25 cents. They were flimsy and forgettable, not even as sturdy as leaves, but it was important to count how many you received.

In 1950 I liked a boy who sat two rows ahead of me, but I was too shy to sign the card I left on his desk. I used to draw his profile day after day during spelling and even today the curve of his cheekbone sticks in my memory. I think we were both outside the swirl—observers, not participants—although I never could have put that into words back then. He seemed lonely and kind. His name might have been Dan.

We were asked to buy an inexpensive present for the Valentine's Day grab bag, and I bought ink. I had spent a lot of time in the stationery store unscrewing all the caps and staring into the bottles of deep color. Green, red, black, blue, I would smell them, being careful not to get ink on my nose. I wrapped the smooth glass bottle in tissue paper and placed it as carefully as an egg among the other gifts, waiting proudly for someone to choose it. Finally a boy ripped the paper off and began to wail, *"Who bought this?"*

I am happy to say that later I stole it back.

Write two pages of something you gave that was not appreciated.

Write two pages of what was supposed to be a fun holiday but wasn't.

᠁

No memory Maybe just saying what it is you can't remember gets the engine to turn over. My father, Lewis Thomas, began his memoir, *The Youngest Science*, with this sentence: "I have always had a bad memory; as far back as I can remember. It's not that I forget things outright; I forget where I put them. I need props. The village I grew up in is gone . . . " and he is launched. Small bits and pieces, but evocative of the boy he was, and the times he grew up in, and it is clear that he begins to remember more and more as he writes. I believe his memoir was written all of a piece: memories of Flushing. So sometimes by stating what you can't remember you begin to remember. Make a virtue of the flaw. You don't have to remember dinner-table conversations to tell the story.

Write two pages of what you don't remember (of course you can).

Childhood memories I had a childhood illness that kept me in bed for several months. I was six or seven and we lived in New Orleans. (It is funny that I have not a single memory of ever being hot.) During this time I turned my bedspread into a flying carpet. I spent hours in the air just above everybody's heads, too high to reach, but close enough to cause wonder and jealousy in all my friends. (My mother used to have flying dreams, but the only place she flew was back and forth between the lions at the New York Public Library on 42nd Street.) To keep me company, I was given a pair of lovebirds whose incessant chatter drove me crazy. When some grown-up discovered the dents on top of the cage (which I routinely pounded in a vain attempt to shut them up) they took the birds away.

It was a good time. My imagination got loose. There was no such thing as television; I had tea and buttered toast with grape jam, lots of fairy tales, and my magic carpet.

Write two pages about being sick in bed.

Write two pages about where you would fly if you could.

Wishing you remembered One afternoon an old friend of mine was going through papers and unearthed a letter he'd saved for thirty years. He was taking stock of his life. He was a world-class physicist, but still he wondered at his own hubris. Here is the letter:

> 22 October 1957
> Paris
>
> Following our recent conversation, there is a point which you can, I think, help me clarify, and after having hesitated, I have now decided to put it to you.
>
> The little thinking I have done for the past ten years has led me to one conclusion: there is only one real problem, namely what is the exact relation of man to the universe.
>
> During that conversation, you stated that you knew very clearly what this relation is. Could you tell me what you mean by that? A little note will do.
>
> With all the best,
> Raymonde

My friend would have been thirty-three at the time of the letter. He had forgotten what he had once thought he knew. He would have given a lot to have remembered what it was, because he certainly didn't know it anymore.

Write two pages of what you are no longer certain of.

Write two pages of an unshakable belief.

What you no longer need to remember I smoked for a long time. Once in a while I start up again, smoke for a month or two (or four) and then stop. The stopping, when it finally arrives, requires no effort, no sacrifice. One minute I'm chain-smoking, the next I'm not. When I'm smoking I can't imagine quitting, and when I've quit I can't imagine starting again. My problem is I never really got over thinking smoking was cool. I taught myself how to French inhale in front of a mirror. I don't really need that particular skill anymore. Nor do I need to strike a match using one hand, sophisticated though that used to seem.

I read an essay in which the writer told of how his father had taught him to fold *The New York Times* the long way, the way that makes it possible to read in a NYC subway. He realized he no longer needed that skill, so hard-won, alas. (I forget why, maybe because of computer screens.) My second husband used to bemoan the fact that everything he knew about a previous lover was no longer necessary, they had broken up, he had married me, and all that expertise about her was going to go to waste. You have to know I looked at him differently after he said that. Even though I was young, I knew something was wrong with this statement. As if knowing someone is the emotional equivalent of skillful driving. As if it would get you somewhere.

> *Write two pages about something someone said that you filed away for future reference.*

> *Write two pages about the moment you knew something was over.*

In the summer we kids used to walk atop a split-rail fence on our way to the beach. It was knotted and crooked and covered with rose bushes, and it took a lot of balance and determination to stay up and not get stung by bees or pricked by thorns. I was good at it, looked forward to it every morning. Now, fifty-five years later, where there used to be a split-rail fence there are brick walls too high to see over, let alone climb. (This is not really an obsolete skill, but one rendered impossible by age.) I never did learn to drive a stick, but I gather most cars are automatic now. I think of the young men in high school whose main claim to fame was their artistry in the make-out department. I wonder if people bother to make out anymore. I hope so. Getting there is half the fun.

Maybe it is 99 percent of the fun.

Write two pages of no fun at all.

Write two pages about a skill painfully acquired and now no longer needed.

Write two pages of what you wish you could still do.

Memory and metaphor Chuck's daughter Hannah is choreographing a dance about memory using flashlights and darkness. This seems to me the perfect metaphor for the way memory does and doesn't work: vivid but disjointed. I confess—everything seems to refer back to me these days, I hope this isn't something I've been doing for years and am only just noticing—that I mostly remember unhappiness, vague uneasiness, as if I'd spent my childhood ankle-deep in standing water. So I'm curious about why I don't have any happy memories and my friend Chuck says, with his customary incisiveness, "You don't ponder happiness."

Ponder sticks in my head. Lovely word. Maybe it comes from *pond,* because of reflection, although Narcissus fell in love with his own good looks and did no further work. So I look it up and it derives from a word that means "to weigh." Never mind. Each time you look at *ponder,* there is that calm round circle of water, you can't get away from it.

Write two pages involving a flashlight.

Write two pages that end with "You can't get away from it."

But all this makes me feel better about a recent conversation in which one of my grown daughters agreed with another of my grown daughters that, between them, they had only one happy memory of childhood.

"Only one!" says my friend Claudette. "And they had to share it!"

Write two pages of something that makes you laugh every time.

four

Structure

Structuring memoir There are as many different kinds of memoir as there are motives for writing one. There is memoir written as pure story: You start at the beginning and end where you are now, a breathless headlong rush through what happened. You can start at the end and look back, or with some middle moment, an event that precipitated change and clarity, or the need for clarity. Put the point of your compass there and start circling: big circles, small circles, overlapping circles. You can put together fragments that contain moments of crisis or confusion or hilarity, or moments that stick in the mind for no apparent reason, and while they may not follow chronology in terms of time, they may make an emotional progression. Ilene Beckerman has written a perfect memoir called *Love, Loss, and What I Wore*, an account of her life illustrated by what she was wearing at important moments. I believe someone else has fashioned a memoir comprised entirely of lists.

When I began writing *Safekeeping*—which is, for lack of a better word, a sort of memoir—I had no idea what I was doing. All I knew was that I couldn't stop. What were these little pieces I was feverishly scribbling? They had started coming a few weeks after an old friend died, a man I'd been married to once upon a time, someone I'd known half my life. The pages piled up. Memories, moments, scenes, nothing longer than a few pages, some only a line or two. There was no narrative flow. There was no narrative at all. But these bits and pieces kept flying out of me, and I kept writing them down. I didn't know if what I was doing would amount to anything, but I never cross-examine the muse.

I left out long boring patches of life I could barely recall. I left out jobs, shrink appointments, lousy boyfriends. I left out a scene that contained two naked people and a scimitar. But I still found plenty to write. I changed voices from first to third when it felt right. I mixed up past and present. There was no chronological sense to it, no order. It was popcorn. The only thing I was sure of was that I would stop with my friend's death. Grief had been the catalyst; grief would be the end.

But I hadn't died. Everywhere around me life went on. My eldest daughter had a daughter, and she named her after me, an honor I didn't feel worthy of. My grandmotherly visit was painful, guilt-ridden, but it contained a miracle, and when I realized that this was where I wanted to end, I began to see a kind of emotional chronology. The pieces tumbled back and forth, but something was evolving.

My editor turned it down. She wanted me to write a *novel* about that marriage, what went wrong, what went right, then friendship, illness, and death. But life doesn't arrange itself conveniently into chapters—not mine, anyway. And I didn't want to write a novel. My life didn't feel like a novel. It felt like a million moments. I didn't want to make anything fit together. I didn't want to make anything up. I didn't want it to make sense the way I understand a novel to make a kind of sense. I didn't want anywhere to hide. I didn't want to be able to duck. I wanted the shock of truth. I wanted moments that felt like body blows. I wanted moments of pure hilarity, connected to nothing that came before or after. I wanted it to feel like the way I've lived my life. And I wanted to tell the truth. My truth doesn't travel in a straight line, it zigzags, detours, doubles back. Most truths I have to learn over and over again.

There is no hard-and-fast rule about structure; you can invent your own. This morning I thought, well, imagine your memoir as a sheet of paper and the structure is like an origami bird you fashion from it. I called my sister Eliza to try this out on her, since her daughter PanPan is a terrific origami maker. "I love her cranes," I said to Eliza. "Isn't it a good metaphor for structure?"

A little pause.

"Well," she said, "one morning I came down and she was surrounded by 500 hopping toads."

Write an ode to a part of your body. You could probably structure an entire memoir using different parts of the human body.

Write two pages about your feet.

Where there's a will My sister Judy suggests that a good way to get going on memoir is to write your will. You have to decide who gets all your treasures, and this involves looking at them, and remembering where you found them. She reminds me that when my youngest daughter, Catherine, was a little girl, Judy took care of her for a week while her father and I went to Mexico. Catherine was fascinated by all Judy's stuff and said, joyfully, "I can't wait for you to die so I can have your things!"

Recently I heard Catherine say to one of her twin boys, as she carried him around my backyard, "Just think! Some day all this will be partially yours!"

A lawyer tells me that when writing your will, the legal term for one's possessions is "the natural objects of my bounty." How lovely that is, implying nothing of getting and spending, nothing that smacks of commercialism.

Write two pages about your treasures.

Write two pages about the unnatural objects of your bounty.

Who would want what's on my mantel? All those little boxes. They are not pretty, and there is nothing inside except beads and lost earrings. I can't imagine anyone wanting the rusty finial of a bird's head. I must remember to tell my family that there is no need to be sentimental. "Treasure" is a subjective term. One of my possessions is a black plastic ashtray filled with a collection of my father's skipping stones. My friend Paul has a collection of manhole covers. ("Don't ask," he says.) Judy tells me, before we're off the phone, "I want my stuff buried with me."

Write two pages of what you can't pass down.

Write two pages about what you want to take with you.

Later Judy tells me that if we come back, she wants to come back as a pebble in a tidal pool, or a minnow swimming around the pebble. "Why not come back as the whole tidal pool?" I suggest. Then I tell her that I have always wanted to be a whole school of fish, to see what it feels like to wheel around in the water.

There is the briefest of pauses. "Typical," my sister says.

Write two pages ending with "That's typical."

More about my sister Judy took me to her favorite store. I saw an art-deco teapot and sugar bowl, and pointed them out to her. "I know," she said, "I love them, but they're twenty-eight dollars."

I bought them, and after a brief scuffle with myself, I presented them to my sister. "Oh, no," she said, but I insisted, happy to discover that now that I'm sixty-five I don't have to have everything.

Write two pages about a scuffle with yourself.

Write two pages about what you don't have to have.

&

Noticing the difference A couple of years ago my sister Judy and I were each given a box of truffles. The tiny print said two pieces contained 310 calories and there were six pieces in each box. We were sitting on the bus headed downtown, quietly doing our calculations: Judy was dividing by two and I was multiplying by three. When she realized what I was doing, a look came over her face that is hard to describe. "I lost all hope for you," she says now. The difference between us could not have been more clearly defined than in that moment. (One of the differences, she would be quick to point out.)

There are those people who can eat one piece of chocolate, one piece of cake, drink one glass of wine. There are even people who smoke one or two cigarettes a week. And then there are people for whom one of anything is not even an option.

Write two pages about when a striking difference between you and another person became clear.

Write two pages that involve memories of chocolate.

There are other basic differences between people. As my friend Chuck pointed out, there are people who go on vacation and count the number of days left in the vacation, and those who count the number of days left until they get to go home. My daughter Jen and I took a trip to Scotland a few years ago. We planned it in advance, and two weeks before we left we began counting the days until we got home. We missed our dogs, but that doesn't really explain it. And it's not that we didn't have a wonderful time. We did.

Write two pages of what goes through your mind while you're packing for a trip.

Write two pages of feeling homesick.

Use specific details Back when I was a literary
agent I received a proposal from a woman named
Virginia Dabney who wanted to write about her
mother's farm, where she had grown up. In her proposal, she wrote about the birds singing outside the
window, and some other things I can't remember.
Nothing caught my attention until she talked about
the cold winters and the unheated house, and how,
to keep her children warm, her mother put newspapers between the sheets and blankets for insula-
tion. Now that was interesting. I wrote her back
saying I didn't want to hear anything about the
beauty of the birdsong, but please tell me more
about those newspapers.

A year later I received a manuscript called
*Once There Was a Farm: A Country Childhood
Remembered*, which was bought and published by
Random House.

Details. Specifics. Eliminate all abstract nouns.

Write two pages of how you kept/keep warm.

Write two pages of details about being cold.

Keep track of what you notice What you look at is part of who you are. Keep an eye on yourself. See where what you notice takes you. There's an old man who sometimes stands on the side of a busy road across from a place that sells mushroom soil and gravel and heaps of black crumbly earth and white pebbles for driveways. Often the lot is filled with big pyramids of one substance or another. In December there are Christmas trees. The man just stands there, staring. He is short and a little fat. What is he doing? What is he watching for? It makes no sense to me. I'm too shy to stop my car and ask.

I want to shift gears now and say I've seen him standing there in all kinds of weather—rain, snow, hot sun—but I'm probably making that up to add drama and mystery. Adding that kind of detail is the way fiction starts its engine—*It was a dark and stormy afternoon and* . . . but I want answers. What on earth is he there for? Is he spying? Waiting for a friend? He doesn't stand in the attitude of waiting. He doesn't look hopeful. He is just staring.

Once I walked up Sixth Avenue with a poet friend. We were standing in front of a flower store, and my friend had his notebook open, scribbling away. Maybe it was a legal pad. The proprietor came out, nervously asking if something was wrong. Was my friend an inspector? An engineer? My friend said no, and explained he was writing a poem. There were unpleasant words of some kind, I can't remember what was said or misunderstood, but the shop owner asked us to move on, and we did. My friend frowned, and whispered his threat: "The poem just changed."

Write two pages of a question you wish you'd asked.

Write two pages of revenge that nobody notices.

Another strange person My daughter-in-law Kirsten told me of a woman seen riding a bicycle somewhere in Montana. She was wearing a tweed skirt and a tweed jacket, not really the right gear for the terrain or the transport. Later, people came upon her bicycle lying at the side of the road and they were alarmed enough to investigate. They found her with a garbage bag over her head, and when they pulled it off she was smoking a cigarette under there. She was terribly annoyed.

Write two pages about finding someone doing something inexplicable.

Write two pages of unwelcome assistance.

⚓

The need for story Recently I went to a conference given by the Brain Injury Association of New York State, and I sat in on a talk given by the director of a traumatic brain injury rehab facility. She said the first thing they do to assist a person who has experienced a loss, not just of memory but of self, is to *make a story*. With the help of family and friends they write a story of the patient's life—the events, names, and faces.

It is basic, our need for story, perhaps because it is such a handy way to carry our experiences around—story as container, so to speak. But the shape can be anything at all. So you can think of your memoir as a soup pot, or a trapeze, or a funnel, and if this helps you, great. What helped me was deciding what my memoir wasn't going to be—it wasn't going to be shackled by chronology.

My advice is to start writing and continue writing. A shape will eventually suggest itself to you. I realize I have said this all before, but I can't emphasize enough that you trust the writing and the shape will appear.

Be sure to include what you can't make fit neatly into your idea of yourself, or whatever it is that ruffles the smooth surface of your life story. Suppose at some point your mother told you that you had a half sister who was ten years older than you. Suppose you discover that you had a brother who died before you were born, and nobody will talk about it, so that piece of information has lain in isolation. Suppose you once discovered love letters in your father's raincoat pocket, and never asked questions. So where does this stuff go? It doesn't fit anywhere. It was a meteor, or a crack, but nothing more came of it. To which I say, well, what is the "anywhere" this doesn't fit? Start there.

Oh, I was just going to skip over all that, you say. Nope. You're going to have to write it.

Write two pages of something you wish you didn't know.

Write two pages of something you regret revealing.

Shapes and sounds I think it was either E. M. Forster or Henry James who described a novel as a big baggy monster. We are talking here only about memoir, but if you could somehow put your entire life into a huge bag, what would be the prevailing sound?

Write two pages that begin with "Get me out of here."

Going through hell The thing about going through hell is that you also have to fry eggs and pay bills and change into pajamas, so hell is usually set against the ordinary living room of your life. Here is ready-made perspective. Write it all down. The hospital rooms, the cries of children, the shopping lists, the phone number for the electrician or the plumber or the tax guy, the visiting hours for family, the visiting hours for friends. Jumble it all together.

Write two pages of jumble.

Motive for memoir Here is as good a place as any to discuss good reasons—and bad ones—for writing memoir. I have mentioned sisters several times already. Those of us with siblings could probably trace our emotional history by chronicling our relationships with our sisters and brothers. There were long periods when my sisters and I did not get along. There were misunderstandings, misappropriations, mistakes. There were the built-in difficulties of birth order. I was the eldest. (Curious that I put that in the past tense. Perhaps I am finally growing up.) If I were to write about my transgressions, or what I once perceived as theirs, and if I came out either as victim or wise old woman, I would be suspicious. I would have to scrap the whole thing.

Memoir is not a place to get revenge, or to appear angelic, or to cast oneself as victim. If that's on your mind, write fiction. Memoir should not be self-serving, even accidentally. If you come out as anything but profoundly human, you've probably got the wrong motives for doing this, or you haven't stood far enough back, or come close enough. If you end up where you started—that is, if you wind up with the same feelings about yourself and your life that you had going into this—well, sometimes memoir is about *this is how it was.* We walked barefoot and upside down to school. We made our own soap, and this is how. That stuff is interesting. Anything you know that I don't (this includes anything that takes place on a farm) is interesting. If I don't know it, I want to.

But poor little me is not a good motive for memoir. Neither is good little me. If that's the point you're setting off to prove, or (even worse) illustrate, you aren't going to get very far.

It's about clarity. Clarity usually involves a good deal more humility than you started out with. And humility is accompanied by generosity. And clarity is dependent on a generosity of vision. I'm not saying we let villains off the hook. There is evil out there. I'm just saying a shift in the way we look at ourselves and our lives is one of the benefits of writing memoir. So keep an open mind, leave room for surprise.

Write two pages of when you failed to rise to the occasion.

🚰

Killing time, or grout for memoir I am killing time waiting for the coffee to brew and the kitchen in this tiny restaurant to open so I can lose half an hour eating lunch while the computer at the hardware store across Tinker Street gets itself together. The nice young man there is letting me store six forty-eight-inch dowels, a gigantic flower pot, and *The New York Times* behind the counter. "It could be a while," he said, when I asked him when the computer might be working again.

"Can't I just give you the exact change?" I asked, but he shook his head. I told him I would come back in half an hour. I said it nicely, but I don't think I was smiling. I wasn't mad, I just wasn't smiling. Didn't feel like it. I believe my expression was neutral.

Earlier, the man laying tile in my bathroom (a job left unfinished because of scheduling difficulties) asked me if I had any grout. "Did you check the basement?" I suggested, and he said there wasn't any down there. "Then I don't have any grout," I answered, leaving the ball in his court. I didn't leap to my feet and offer to go buy him some, which I might have done in my younger years, making up to him for the fact that he didn't have any grout either, and he was the one laying the tile. Nor did I ask, "Do I look like I have any grout?" which was another possible response.

So now twelve minutes have gone by and these are the scribbled notes I have been making in my diary. I apologize for how boring they are, but I notice that when my mind wanders aimlessly around, it often returns to manners in one form or another. This can vary from saying "Please" and "Thank you" and chewing with my mouth closed, to feeling apologetic for difficulties beyond my control and not of my making. Guilt is doubtless part of this. Guilt and manners—a provocative place to begin mulling over a life.

Could I somehow divide my life into sections of overly polite, even obsequious, responses to the universe? If I were writing memoir, I might consider such a thing, especially since the older I get the less inclined I am to feel responsible for the success or failure of somebody else's dinner party. I could think about the history of my life as manifested in manners and/or guilt, the evolving (or devolving) thereof. Think of manners as grout. The point is, again, that even when you're just doodling around, you're writing. You're filling your larder. You're building the shelves. Trust the work to find its own way. Thank you very much for reading this.

Write two pages of what you no longer feel guilty about.

Write two pages about what you feel even guiltier about.

On the other hand, why be so serious? Why not simply record the life you've lived? Growing up sixty-five years ago was vastly different from nowadays. For instance, nobody had invented television when I was little. We didn't have iPods or BlackBerrys or cell phones.

We got to climb trees. We got to read. We got to play in the mud.

Write two pages that end with "Ha ha."

I couldn't finish my lunch. It was healthy in an uninteresting way. "No thank you," I said to the waitress, "don't wrap it up." It wasn't her fault. I left a big tip.

Further thoughts about manners My aunt Rhoda, who never married, was fond of saying that more marriages were ruined by bad table manners than by infidelity. I was married three times, and I must say that infidelity was right up there at the top of the list, right next to sucking soup through one's teeth.

Write two pages of what you learned to overlook.

Write two pages of what you could not overlook.

🖋

All right, table manners I eat with a large spoon. I eat everything with a large spoon. If I were sitting across the table from me, I'd have to look away. I have only the vaguest notion of how horrible this must appear to the casual observer. After all, the purpose of a large spoon is to get as much on it and then into my mouth as possible. My mother was a stickler for good manners. "Napkin in the lap," she would say, snapping her fingers. When passing the salt, put it down on the table; never let it be taken from your hand directly. Why not? Bad luck!

Which brings me to superstition. My family was rife with superstition. To this day I do not stir anything with a knife, or rock an empty rocking chair, or say anything or anybody is perfect, at least not without touching wood. I have learned to pass the salt directly from my hand to another's, although I do always throw some over my left shoulder if it spills. The day I found out that if you do not put the salt down you will have to fight a duel, I lost interest. When the consequences were spelled out like that, they didn't really bother me anymore.

Write two pages of family superstitions.

Write two pages of pretending to like the food.

Bad manners We weren't supposed to cut all our meat at once. We were supposed to cut one piece, eat that, then cut another. Why? Never mind. I am already weary of the subject.

Write two pages about good manners that make no sense.

Write two pages in which your enthusiasm rapidly waned.

Ideal day My notion of what constitutes an ideal day has changed over time. Here is one from now. I can't remember ten years ago. Not yet, anyway.

It is March 2, 2007. Outside the sleet is coming down. Inside I have a fire in the fireplace, and chicken soup on the stove, almost ready for the dumplings to go in. My dog Rosie got hurt on a wire fence on Monday and she has a dozen stitches, and a regimen of no activity until the day after tomorrow. She isn't even supposed to climb stairs. I had to take Carolina and Harry to a doggie sleep-away for a few days, the three of them together are too rambunctious. So here I am—bad weather, no duties, and an armful of warm dog. Nobody expects anything of me. Nobody even knows I'm here, because I'm supposed to be somewhere else. For me, this is heaven, pure and simple.

It is quiet. I hadn't realized how noisy Carolina is—she is a hound and it is in her nature to pursue every lead. When she gets up howling—every fifteen minutes or so—Rosie and Harry follow suit, so as not to appear slackers. The peace and quiet is soothing, but I couldn't live this way for long.

Write two pages of a sudden silence.

I am supposed to be in Atlanta at a writers' conference and although I had looked forward to it, there was no doubt in my mind that my first responsibility was to my dog. Still, it took me a while to cancel. It wasn't that I was going to go, I wasn't. It wasn't that I preferred Atlanta to Rosie, I didn't. But some part of me just couldn't undo my flight, or my hotel room, or my part in the conference (very small). I drove myself crazy. What was wrong with me? Why didn't I get it over with? Finally I did, and I felt better, and after the dust settled I realized what had stopped me. Alone in a new city, hobnobbing with my fellow goblins, it was an adventure. I wasn't ready to stop wondering what it would be like.

Write two pages about your ideal day—one for each decade.

Write two pages of putting off relief.

One last thing. When I first found Rosie stuck and bleeding, I wanted some other person to come and be the responsible party, to take her off the wire, to examine the extent of her injuries, to get her to the hospital. But there was nobody but me out there, and Rosie is my dog. My friend Claudette drove us to the vet. She said she hated to look at injuries too, which made me feel marginally better about myself.

Write two pages of a responsibility you'd rather have ducked.

Monday night, after I got Rosie home, I ate two pints of ice cream, one after the other. The first was because she was home and going to be all right. The second was because she'd been injured in the first place.

Controlling the details Suppose you are writing about a woman sitting down at her table to eat supper. Suppose her husband has died, and this is the first time she's had to face his empty chair. Suppose she went grocery shopping earlier in the afternoon. Maybe she did several errands; she picked up some dry cleaning, bought a book. Maybe you include these details, maybe you don't. Let's look at the choices.

If you list everything she bought at the market, the bread, butter, sugar, the tomatoes and pasta, the dog food, and then you describe her putting everything away carefully, you might be doing it for one of two reasons. You might want to show that she is reluctant to go home, so you linger with her over every choice, you show the reader that she is taking longer about this than she might otherwise have done. You don't have to say right out that she is putting off returning to an empty house as long as she can. The empty house is there in the background. Make sure the rhythm of language is working. Say the sentences out loud. Maybe you want the rhythm to represent a tumbling downhill. If you are in control of the language, you can do anything. But if you are listing her purchases because you feel like it, or because you are in the habit of stuffing details into everything, you will probably have to say out loud that she is lonely. This means the writing is failing. This means, possibly, that the details are in there only because you are obsessive about detail. That's not a good enough reason. You will bury the moment under the heap of groceries. You want the moment of her sitting down alone to be the point. You want the reader to ache as she aches. All you need is to have her look at his empty chair.

Or maybe she is celebrating. Maybe she is glad her husband had died, maybe he was a terrible selfish boring old coot, maybe he abused her in various ways. Maybe he was mean to her, mean to his children. Then this meal is a different kind of occasion, she cooks herself something special. She raises a glass of wine to his empty chair.

Or maybe the way you portray loneliness is to be spare in your language—the lonely unadorned sentence. She took the long way home. It was dark when she pulled into the driveway. She fed the dogs and scrambled herself a couple of eggs. Maybe she notices the clinking sound her fork makes on the plate. The point is you shouldn't have to say anything about her emotions. This is that old chestnut: *Show, don't tell*. Of course, it is also possible to tell and make that work too, but I don't know how to do that.

What, you may ask, does dramatization have to do with memoir? Surely this is more the stuff of fiction. Writing is writing, and the reader will be more engaged if allowed to feel without being told what to feel. Trusting the reader provides a tension that keeps the writer engaged too.

Write two pages (or less) of a single woman's shopping list.

Write two pages in which you are reluctant to go home.

&

Light Different memoirs require different voices. If you are writing about your autistic child, you are writing as a mother. If you are recalling an untimely death, you write from loss. When I wrote *A Three Dog Life*, which is a book about my husband's traumatic brain injury, I was writing as his wife. I wasn't writing as the mother of four, or the grandmother of twelve; I wasn't writing about my relationship to my own parents, or to my sisters, or my friends, I was writing as

Rich's wife. That is the lens through which I looked at what was happening; both of us were changed and changing. There were aspects of myself I'd prefer never to have uncovered, but memoir will do that.

Catastrophe brings out the best and the worst. That's the deal, and everything goes into the mix, good and bad. On the whole, I'd say it's easier to know oneself than to fool oneself, and it requires less energy.

If it can't be forgiven, at least it can be brought up to the light.

five

Writing from Loss

Make something out of it Writing is a way to fathom what we have lost, to make sense out of what makes no sense. This section is about losses of all kinds. I don't believe that everything happens for a reason, but I have faith in our ability to retrieve from loss something valuable to keep, or to give away. In writing *A Three Dog Life*, I had to examine a subject I thought myself too sophisticated to be troubled with—survivor guilt. In tossing around for some way to feel okay about the fact that I was alive and well, I looked up the word *acceptance*, and found that in part of its DNA is an ancient cousin that means "a thread used in weaving." Sometimes the language itself holds an answer. You must weave in the thread and keep on weaving.

Lost objects, lost childhood, lost dreams, lost innocence. Lost loved ones. Here is a group of exercises that deal with both the trivial and the profound.

What we cannot lose Maybe there are those of us who need our props: our books in our bookcases, our pillows, our chairs and doodads, our kitchen sinks. Maybe if we are too long away, we lose sense of who we are, we are ungrounded. There is a passage in *So Long, See You Tomorrow*, a novel by William Maxwell, in which he talks of a boy sent away from home, and he lists the things that are no longer in this boy's life: "Take all this away and what have you done to him? In the face of a deprivation so great, what is the use of asking him to go on being the boy he was. He might as well start life over again as some other boy instead."

Write two pages of what would have to be taken away to make you no longer who you are.

Write two pages of what you don't need.

Loss of time When I was young, and for a long time afterward, Sunday afternoons were melancholy. I used to blame it on memories of my father retiring alone to his study to listen to classical music. I didn't like classical music. It made me uneasy. I liked Carl Perkins and Elvis Presley and Ray Charles. I liked Bobby Darin and Buddy Holly. I didn't understand music you couldn't sing or dance to, and there was something about him holed up in there all by himself that depressed me. I didn't like the closed door.

But I think something else was going on. The span of a week is a reminder of the finite, even to the young. And powerful Sunday, which starts out fat and lazy, stretching endlessly ahead, dwindles to a wisp, and just like that, it's over.

Write two pages about your relationship to Sundays, in ten-year intervals.

Write two pages of your relationship to Saturdays, ditto.

Loss of sleep I have a friend who went to another city to sleep. He had insomnia and he had tried everything else. I have no trouble sleeping, my problem is staying awake, but I went along for the ride. We flew to New Orleans, where I hadn't been since I was eight years old. We ate beignets and fried oysters. We stayed in a large hotel. As it turned out, the city was full of football fans. LSU was playing Oklahoma (was it Oklahoma?) in one of the college-bowl playoffs. Purple pom-poms everywhere. Nothing looked familiar to me and he still couldn't get to sleep.

Write two pages of taking extreme measures.

Write two pages of insomniac thoughts.

My friend lives with something that kills you. He jokes about it, and most of the time I forget how serious it is. He's the person I call when something hilarious happens, or something scares me to death. He is the person I rely on to keep me sane and honest. He is wise and terribly funny. My fears for him are selfish. It's not his death I fear so much as my life without him.

Write two pages of a selfish fear.

Loss of identity On a recent plane ride I sat next to an elderly gentleman. He was friendly and pleasant, and he engaged me in conversation. The plane was noisy, and he asked me what I did and I replied, "I'm a writer." He asked me how long I had been a waiter and I said since I was forty-eight. I caught on to his misunderstanding when he began to tell me about his favorite restaurant in Albany, but I didn't correct him. When I asked him what he did, I thought he said he was an elevator engineer, but later I gathered that he was in elementary education—a principal, as it turned out. He had had a long and satisfying career.

We had a pleasant journey. If I were writing fiction, I might have written a story about it.

Write two pages of a mistake you didn't bother to correct.

Momentary loss of desire to be close to a creature you love My son Ralph recently installed a dog door for us, and today as I sat unraveling a knitting project gone wrong, Rosie hopped up on the pillow behind me. When I'd gotten all of what had started out as sweater back into one big ball of yarn, I turned to look at my dog and discovered to my horror that we were both covered with bird feathers.

It took forever to get the feathers off us, off the chair, and off the floor. There was no other debris, thank god.

Write two pages of the downside of something or someone you love.

Write two pages in which you overreacted.

Carolina, my third hound, had been carrying a dead squirrel around the yard for two days, like a child with a favorite toy. I was horrified, but my son said, "She's so proud of it," which changed my feelings, but only slightly. I approached her as she lay on the grass, the squirrel between her paws. She growled—a friendly growl, but a growl nonetheless.

I am not stupid. When she came into the house for supper (sans squirrel) I went outside, found it, and tossed the poor dead thing into the bushes, out of reach. After supper she searched for a long time.

Write two pages of someone you love holding something you don't.

∕

Lost objects Recently I lost something that belongs to someone else, something precious. She has asked for it back and I haven't told her yet that I can't find it because I'm waiting to turn the house upside down. Until I've looked everywhere, there is still a chance it may turn up. I think I last saw it in a bag that contained a scarf I was knitting for my grandson Dan. That is lost too. Dan picked out the blue wool himself.

What is wrong with me?

If I were younger, I would probably turn against the person whose treasure disappeared. *It's her fault for loaning it to me in the first place.* I would have thought. *I didn't ask to see it . . .*

So I suppose I've made progress. But I still can't find it.

Write two pages of blaming the injured party.

∕

Loss of a dream A red chicken coop is slowly falling apart in a corner of my yard. It's still winter, so the red coop has white snow on its roof, but lacking the white chickens, not much depends on this. The windows are broken, the lattice that served some unknown purpose has sagged to the ground and is in the process of disintegrating. I've lived up here four years and been inside the chicken coop twice. I recall seeing a big sign for a real estate business, and a bunch of storm windows. Recently my son-in-law discovered an old suitcase full of pornography but he left it in the coop. There are flagstones in front of the low entrance to the place, and when it gets warm if you lift them up carefully you can find a few little newts underneath. In summer the forsythia is so dense and high that the coop is hard to get to—or hard to get to if you're thinking about deer ticks or snakes, or other varmints wilder than my three dogs, who can spend hours barking at those bushes.

In the old days I used to get that wonderful recurring dream where you stumble on a room in your house you didn't know was there. It's always a spare room, and you half-remember it, and you realize it is the perfect place to do the things or think the thoughts you've always meant to do or think, but lacked the right chair in the right room, with the right light—and here it is, in this room you've always had. I don't have those dreams anymore, but I think it's because I have a house with many rooms, and this real chicken coop I could fix up given some inspiration and a potful of found money. Sometimes I even think—briefly—of keeping a bunch of chickens. One street over someone has a rooster. We could get together.

> *Write two pages of the perfect room for the perfect activity (or lack thereof).*

> *Write two pages of old dreams you miss.*

Loss of self-respect One summer years ago I was working alone in an office that was also somebody's apartment. I was the only one there. The walls were dark green in the room where I worked, and I was lonely, so I called my sister Eliza in Boston every day, and we talked for hours. A small part of me felt uneasy, maybe I shouldn't be doing this, but I kept on anyway. When my boss got back she opened her telephone bill, and flabbergasted, she asked if I knew whose number had the 617 exchange. Cornered, I lied. "I don't know," I said. That night I went home and called all my children. *It's okay, Ma, it's not so terrible, Ma, someday this will be a funny story, Ma,* they all said. But it was clear to all of us that I needed to tell the truth and pay her back. I wrote a check for the money I'd talked away, and confessed.

The worst was that I had failed to live up to my own expectations. I was not the person I'd taken myself to be—someone who would tell the truth no matter the consequences. I looked in the mirror and saw a coward. For some reason, the thieving part wasn't nearly as humiliating. It is a funny story now, but only because I've forgiven myself, a process that took years. I had to come to the liberating realization that I was human.

Is there a moment when you failed yourself? I have many shameful moments, but most of them were instances in which I failed other people. Moments, no, years, when I had no clear idea who I was hoping to be, just that I was a miserable failure. (What is a mother, anyway?)

Write two pages of lies.

Write two pages of a lie you were told.

At a loss for words I was watching *Prime Suspect* last night, and Helen Mirren has to break the news of a boy's suicide to his parents. I wonder how can she bear to do this, and even though this is only television, I can hardly watch. And then it hits me. There are these three things in her office: the boy's parents, Helen herself, and the awful truth. And the truth has its rights. Poor Helen has no respectable choice, she can't shirk this responsibility. The truth is there, stark, irrefutable, and there is no way to make it change its shape.

Does this make the bad news easier to deliver? I'm trying to remember delivering bad news, but my mind goes blank. I only remember hearing it, so I can't vouch for the comfort.

The other day I received a piece of unpleasant news from a young man who was lighting a cigarette. I took the damn thing from his hand, had a drag, then lit my own. Amazing how easily the great dark god of nicotine wakes up in my bloodstream. I can see him lying lazily on one side, beckoning. *Where have you been?*, I hear him say. *What took you so long?* He is a constant lover.

Write two pages of bad news.

Write two pages of wrong comfort.

Loss of a clear definition of heaven and hell My friend Sarah sent me a list of hells she found in an old book in the library at Notre Dame University. It included the following version of hell: "slipping and falling on a path of well-oiled beans." I must remember to ask her when the book was last taken out.

Write two pages of your version of hell.

Write two pages of your childhood version of hell.

I don't know when I realized that you couldn't fly to heaven on a plane. I had assumed that if the plane could get high enough, there it would be. Clouds had a lot to do with this, because that's where I pictured God and his angels hanging out. This was before anyone I knew died, so I didn't have the general public up there. At this moment I am flying above some fluffy clouds, imagining a few old friends waving to me as the plane goes by. They are wearing their civilian clothes. My father is among them. He is wearing a suit and tie. I can't see Rich.

Write two pages of a wave that signifies both hello and good-bye.

Loss of strength I've had three private Pilates lessons. Last night I used my abdominal muscles to get me out of a tight spot—I was wedged crookedly between three dogs, and experiencing a searing pain in my back. My abdomen used to be as tight as a drum; it was the source of all my strength. It occurs to me that I gave away more money when my stomach muscles worked, although I can't explain that. My neck is killing me and I can't turn my head from side to side without screaming. I find it hard to reach my shoulder blades. This is due to my sleeping habits, not my new exercise regime. If you lie down with dogs, sometimes you can't get up at all.

Write two pages entitled "The Source of My Strength."

I have arthritis in one hip, and sometimes it is hard to walk. The word *arthritis* stunned me. This was not part of the plan.

Write two pages about the loss of mobility.

Loss of serenity I don't know why bad news always comes as a surprise. By now we should know better. There you are, pleasantly floating in the blue water on a summer day, not a blip on the horizon, and then, suddenly, an oil tanker is bearing down on you and your flimsy little pair of water wings.

Write two pages of what comes next, and how to like it.

Loss of humor Sometimes I lose my sense of humor. My children are usually the first to point this out, which doesn't help restore it.

Write two pages of what you no longer find funny.

Loss of control Ah, happiness. It comes and goes unbidden—one day there it is, wafting through the open window, and then one day there isn't. I don't know what our founding fathers were thinking. You can't pursue happiness.

Write two pages of baiting a trap.

Write two pages of being caught in a trap.

Loss of regime I don't drink, and I don't drink for good reason, but tonight I had two glasses of red wine. It was my son's wine, not mine. I didn't buy it. He drank his with the lamb stew I made. I drank mine with a pint of chocolate ice cream. We watched *The Bourne Conspiracy*. I'm awake now, and it's two-thirty in the morning. I can go downstairs and look for the cigarette I've got hidden and smoke it.

Okay. Did that. Now I have several choices. The first is to decide that a couple of glasses of wine have already started me down the slippery slope and I might as well finish the bottle. The second is that since I only had two glasses I can now drink moderately (and might as well finish the bottle). The third is that I can jump in my car and drive to Cumberland Farms and buy a pack of cigarettes and come back and finish the bottle. The last is okay I enjoyed the stuff, now let's move on.

I think I will regard tonight as a pleasant interlude in a long life of sobriety that stretches ahead.

Or a short one, you never know.

Write two pages of what you didn't plan to do.

Write two pages of the vices you no longer have.

Death I've caught two glimpses of my father, dead these many years, once crossing a street in Midtown, once through the window of a magazine store, and both times I suffered the shock of his death all over again. My old friend Quin told me he hadn't really understood his father was dead until he started to see him in subways.

My husband, Rich, died January 1, 2007. Months went by before it hit me. At first my sorrow was more for what had happened to his life than for his death. Sadness, yes, I was prepared for that, but not the kind of grief that clobbers you, the kind that ambushes you when you're walking down the tea-and-coffee aisle at the market. I had the distinct feeling I was getting away with something— I wasn't going to feel anything worse than what I had already gone through. Hadn't I spent the last seven years grieving?

I can't remember the exact moment. At first there were little things that got to me. When I paid the bill for the ambulance service that took Rich to the hospital for what turned out to be the last time. When I went to gather the few things from Rich's room at the nursing home, and signing in at the front desk I realized that in the space where you put the person you are visiting, I had no one to put. But even though I was crying, that huge grief was still at bay.

Then one day I found myself looking at old photographs of Rich, really looking. I hadn't allowed myself to remember who he had been, who we had been together, and there we were smiling at the camera a few weeks after we were married. There was the steady good man I'd fallen in love with years ago. I'd forgotten how handsome he was, and how happy we were, and the grief that had been eluding me (or that I had been eluding) finally arrived. The strange thing is that I am grateful for it. I realize what I lost.

How are you doing?, a friend asks. I had taken care of Rich for so long, she said, what was I doing to fill that empty space? My friend didn't mouth platitudes; she has suffered her own losses. I didn't want to hear *Everything happens for a reason*. I didn't want to hear *His death must be a blessing*. The space Rich occupied is empty. It will always be empty. Every time I come to the road that leads to the nursing home, my car automatically changes lanes to make the turn. We are creatures of habit.

Write two pages of what waits in ambush.

Write two pages of what you don't want to hear.

Use it or lose it Sometimes you wake up at four in the morning with all this energy and no cows to milk. So you just have to get up and figure out what it's there for. Use it or lose it. If you're lucky some part of you will know what to do, but it's not the part that thinks it's steering. Make sure you have your notebook and a pen.

Who are we and why does it matter? If you are doing the exercises, you are going to have a larder full of material. If there is a common thread, follow it. If you return again and again to a specific time or place, set up a tent there. If you are still plagued by the question of who is going to find it interesting, please remember that most of us are curious about each other's lives. My rule of thumb is that if you find something interesting, chances are good that it *is* interesting.

Who are we? We are mothers, fathers, sons and daughters, sisters, brothers. We are plumbers, lawyers, homemakers. We have waited tables, we have worked in hospitals. We are masons and secretaries and middle managers and bank tellers. We have sold books, we have sold shoes, we have managed produce departments in big supermarkets, we are engineers and soldiers and police and musicians and scientists. We are teachers. We are comedians and volunteers. We are executives, customer service representatives, carpenters, clerks, babysitters, writers, editors, fishermen, inventors. We have worn high heels and construction boots and gray suits and overalls and pocket protectors.

We have spoken from experience, we have talked through our hats. We have been thanked, we have been humiliated, we have gossiped and worried and gone to bed hungry for one thing or another. We have been paranoid, we have had faith. We have been frightened, we have given comfort. We have been unfairly blamed, we have been unjustly praised, we have protested and we have kept our mouths shut. We have bragged and we have sold ourselves short. We have believed lies, hidden our feelings, scrutinized our motives. We have followed every lead; we have turned our faces away. We have been generous to a fault, we have guarded our treasures. We have gone out on a limb and we have stayed on the porch.

We are full of contradiction and conflict; we have played different roles at different times (or simultaneously); we have evolved out of many different selves. Writing memoir is one way to explore how you became the person you are. It's the story of how you got here from there.

Believe me. It's a good story.

six

More Exercises

Note: The two-page part is a tic, you can write more or less.

Assignments:

    —Write two pages of apologies (I once mistyped this as twenty-two pages of apologies).

    —Write two pages of instructions to the child you once were.

    —Write two pages about a tic.

—*Write two pages about an unwelcome surprise.*

—*Write two pages in which something is broken.*

—*Write two pages about a stomachache.*

—*Write two pages about homesickness for somewhere you never were.*

—*Write two pages in which something is too small.*

—*Write two pages that take place in the woods.*

—*Write two pages about a proposal of marriage.*

—*Write two pages about a jinx.*

—*Write two pages of a tantrum you regret.*

—Write two pages of begging for something you don't really need.

—Write two pages of finding something awful in the cellar.

—Write two pages of being afraid of the attic.

—Write two pages about a bad haircut.

—Write two pages in which a spider plays a prominent role.

—Write two pages of a thank-you letter you don't mean a word of.

—Write two pages about a music lesson you didn't want.

—Write two pages about being discovered doing something you'd rather have had remain secret.

—*Write two pages about an untrainable animal.*

—*Write two pages about making the bed.*

—*Write two pages about giving a dog a bath.*

—*Write two pages, the last line of which is, "That's my story and I'm sticking to it."*

—*Write two pages about scolding a child.*

—*Write two pages of something that doesn't get better.*

—*Write two pages that end, "But she came back."*

—*Write two pages in which you were unmasked.*

—*Write two pages about sitting in someone's lap.*

—*Write two pages of being too cold.*

—Write two pages of being too hot.

—Write two pages of something vanished.

—Write two pages in which you do something wrong that you do not regret.

—Write two pages of taking your time.

—Write two pages of an irritating sound you can't locate the source of.

—Write two pages that begin, "That's enough of that."

—Write two pages that end, "That's enough of that."

—Write two pages in which someone fell down.

—Write two pages that begin, "That's not yours."

—Write two pages of fighting about food.

—*Write two pages in which someone fails
to move something too heavy.*

—*Write two pages of making a silk purse
out of a sow's ear.*

—*Write two pages of something you expected
to turn out differently.*

—*Write two pages in which someone throws
her weight around.*

—*Write two pages that begin, "There are
many things I miss."*

—*Write two pages in which you are suddenly
not afraid.*

—*Write two pages of a man crying in another
room.*

—*Write two pages of instructions on how to
kill flies.*

—Write two pages the second sentence of which is, "It's not funny."

—Write two pages in which a child comforts an adult.

—Write two pages in which someone kills something by accident.

—Write two pages about looking for a lost animal.

—Write two pages that take place in a waiting room.

—Write two pages that end, "And that's the story."

—Write two pages of something you vowed never to forget that you forgot.

—*Write two pages in which someone runs out of matches.*

—*Write two pages of Notes to Self.*

—*Write two pages in which someone throws and misses.*

—*Write two pages that end, "I could go on and on."*

A Note About the Series

Thinking About Memoir is the first volume in an ongoing series on the arts of living that AARP Books will publish over the next few years. The series is intended to provoke thinking about some of the personal and public disciplines and graces that have fallen into disuse in our recent history: such virtues as civility, conversation, listening, courage, loyalty, remembering, patience, and love.

Now that we all expect to live twenty years or more beyond the traditional "retirement age," we're going to have to do some work on ourselves. It takes more than sound finances, an exercise plan, and a pleasant climate (useful as these are) to face down the chronic conditions of old age. We need to make ourselves emotionally and intellectually fit for the voyage. To survive, as individuals and as a culture, we're going to have to learn the arts of living.

Living is said to be an art, and like any art it must be practiced with diligence (to paraphrase Dr. Johnson) before it can be done with ease. There is nothing we do in our everyday lives that could not be done with greater understanding. Our practice is in every case a twofold benefit—for ourselves and for the public weal.

Very few learned this while still young. Most of us spent the first half or more of our lives trying to provide for our families and ourselves. It's only in the later, latter half that the questions come: What must I do, how shall I live, what difference will my life have meant when I have come to its end?

All of the arts of living depend on learning to pay disciplined attention to some aspect of the world. These books address the notion of excellence—the idea, oddly lacking in our time, that one can set out to perfect oneself at any age. The greatest and most indispensable of all human enterprises, the "examined life," can be attended to at any moment. The books in our series aim to provide a point of entry to that singular adventure. More is at stake than our individual happiness, for each person is also a cell in the larger body politic; our enduring as a culture, even as a species, may be in question.

Index